Crochet for Beginners

The Most Exhaustive Step By Step Guide With

Picture illustrations To Learn Crocheting

CW00829275

EMILY CHIEN

Contents

Introduction

Crochet is a type of needlework that involves interlocking yarn loops with a hooked needle. You can use crochet to make garments, accessories, home decor, and even stuffed toys!

There are a wide variety of yarns and hooks available, but beginners tend to work best with yarns and hooks that they can easily control. Worsted weight is a good choice, and lighter colors can help with figuring out where to insert the hook as you crochet.

Before you begin your first project, it's a good idea to practice your skills and read a few patterns. This will help you understand how the pattern is written, and will also allow you to see if you have any trouble with any stitches or techniques.

Almost all patterns are split into parts, so you should always read through the instructions in order to follow each part of the pattern. In addition, it's a good idea to have a notebook or pencil with you so that you can note down any abbreviations or symbols used in the pattern. This will save you from having to refer back to the pattern later on, which is especially important if you're new to crochet.

Once you've mastered the basic stitches, it's time to move onto the next step in learning how to crochet: learning to increase and decrease. This will help you to create more complex and interesting projects, such as amigurumi, which is one of the most popular forms of crochet today.

To begin the process, you'll want to learn how to make a slip knot. This is the first stitch you'll need to master and will be useful for many different crochet projects.

After making the slip knot, you'll need to learn how to hold your hook and yarn in a way that feels comfortable for you. Most people hold their crochet hook in the same hand that they use to crochet, but you can also try holding it with your non-dominant hand if you prefer.

You may also need to learn how to work in rows, which will help you to make more complicated projects. A great way to practice working in rows is to make a swatch of the number of stitches and rows specified in your pattern. This will ensure that you'll have the same number of stitches and rows as the pattern, so your finished item will be the same size.

The YO, or yarn over, is another important stitch you'll need to learn. This will be the easiest and fastest stitch you'll ever learn, so it's worth getting used to!

Now that you've learned how to make a slip knot, you should practice it with every stitch you learn. You'll also need to learn how to chain, work a double crochet, and make your first single crochet.

Chapter 1: Basics of Crochet

Crochet is a wonderful way to use a single tool to create a variety of different items, including bags & purses, garments, drink coasters, blankets, pillows, heirlooms and stuffed dolls. It is also a fun and very easy craft to learn.

To get started with crochet, you need a hook and some yarn. Yarn is a very important aspect of the craft and can be anything from very thin thread to bulky wool, but it's best to start with medium average-weight yarn. It's also a good idea to make sure you have some scissors or an X-Acto knife for cutting yarn and threading needles.

The first step is to learn how to hold your hook and yarn correctly. This will take a little practice but once you've mastered it, crocheting will be much easier for you.

You will also need to know how to read a crochet pattern. Many patterns use a variety of abbreviations that you may not be familiar with, so it's worth reading the instructions carefully to make sure you understand what they mean.

Stitches that are commonly used with crochet include chain, single crochet, half double crochet and double crochet (a term for multiple stitches worked in one stitch). All of these basic crochet stitches can be combined to create beautiful and unique patterns, but each of them has its own distinct characteristics.

Chain

The chain stitch is the most basic of all crochet stitches and is necessary for most of your first projects. It is also referred to as a foundation chain and will appear between other stitches on the row or round you're working on.

Sc – Slip Knot

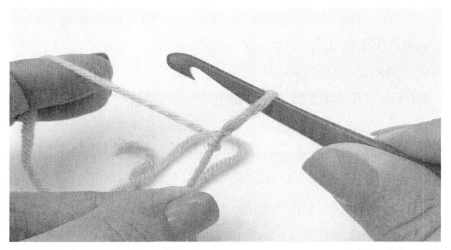

The slip knot is the second most important stitch to learn in crochet, as it secures your yarn to your hook. Once you have learned how to slip knot, you can move on to making chains and other more complex stitches.

It's a good idea to practice these basic crochet stitches on something small before you work on a larger project, such as a scarf. This will help you to build confidence and make sure you're using the right technique.

WS/RS – Wrong Side/Right Side

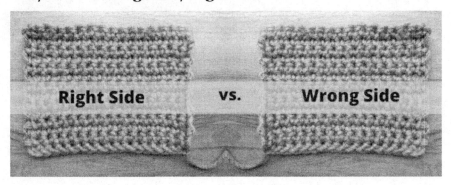

The wrong side of the fabric refers to the side that is facing you, while the right side of the fabric refers to the side of the project you're working on. This is very important as it can prevent you from twisting the fabric.

Increasing and Decreasing

These two techniques can be very useful for creating a range of different shapes in your crochet pieces. This is particularly useful for shawls, where they can be used to create triangles and circular shawls, but you can also use these techniques to make squares, rectangular scarves and other shapes.

Crochet Shell Stitches

The shell stitch is an extremely popular crochet stitch, with variations across the board. They are often worked in rows, but can be worked in the round as well. The resulting shells can vary in size and shape depending on the number of stitches worked into them.

A Beginner's Guide to Crochet

Crochet is a fabric-making craft that uses a hook to loop yarn into different patterns. It is a form of textile art that can be used to make clothing, accessories, toys, and home decor. It is a popular hobby for children and adults of all ages.

What Is Crochet?

Crochet can be a great way to pass the time and relax while doing something creative. It is also a good exercise for your brain and can be a stress-free activity for those who are prone to anxiety.

What Are the Basic Tools Needed for Crocheting?

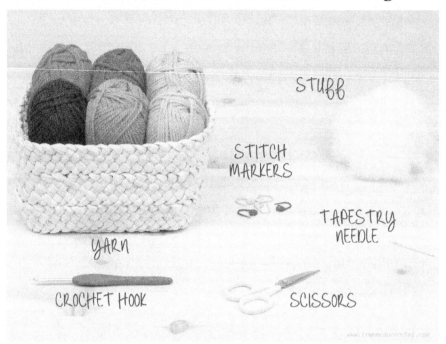

STUFF

STITCH MARKERS

TAPESTRY NEEDLE

YARN

CROCHET HOOK

SCISSORS

The basic tools needed to crochet include a crochet hook, yarn or thread, and stitch markers. Other tools may be required depending on the pattern.

Generally, yarn is available in balls or skeins (hanks), with a yarn band labeling the weight, length, fiber content, dye lot, washing instructions, and recommended needle size for each type of yarn. Many advanced crocheters also choose to use recycled materials such as plastic bags, old t-shirts, and sheets for their work.

Yarn can be purchased from most craft stores and from online retailers, with prices varying by type of yarn. It is best to shop around and try different brands before buying a specific brand.

A wide variety of yarn is available for crocheting, with a selection ranging from mercerized cotton to synthetic and plant and animal-based fibers. Generally, natural fibers are preferred, as they can be more durable and washable.

Some of the most common yarns for crochet are cotton, wool, acrylic, and bamboo. These can be found in a wide range of colors and styles.

What are the Abbreviations Used in Crochet Patterns?

Almost every crochet pattern uses abbreviations to simplify the instructions. This can be helpful if you're new to the craft and want to quickly understand what a pattern is asking for. Often these abbreviations are included in the pattern itself, or a link to a full list is provided on the pattern page.

What is the Difference Between US and UK Crochet Stitches?

The most common crochet stitches are US-style single crochet (sc) and double crochet (dc). The two stitches have a similar appearance, but US-style crochet stitches produce a thicker, more like knit garter stitch fabric, while UK-style crochet stitches produce a thinner, more like slip stitch fabric.

Decreases are another important aspect of crocheting that can be difficult to understand if you've never tried it before. Most crochet decreases require that the first stitch to be decreased is worked until only two loops remain, and then a new stitch is worked into those two loops.

This can be done by wrapping the first loop of the stitch with the hook before working into the next stitch along, or by inserting the hook into the front and back loops of the stitch before working into the top of the stitch. This can create different textures and structures, such as the ribbing commonly found in a crochet scarf.

Essential Crochet Tools Every Beginner Should Have

There are a few essential crochet tools every beginner should have. They're great for helping to keep your projects organized, and can make a big difference in the quality of your crochet work!

Yarn

One of the most fun and exciting things about crochet is picking out the perfect yarn for your project. From baby yarn to super chunky, there's a skein of yarn out there that's perfect for whatever you're making!

Crochet hooks

You'll want to have a variety of different crochet hooks in different sizes as your skill level progresses. You can choose from aluminum, wood, plastic, or ergonomic hooks that are made to be easy on the hands and allow for maximum comfort and control when holding a crochet hook.

A hook case

This is a convenient way to store your crochet hooks when you're not using them. The hooks will stay neat and tidy inside the case, and there are pockets to hold your tape measures and needles.

Stitch markers

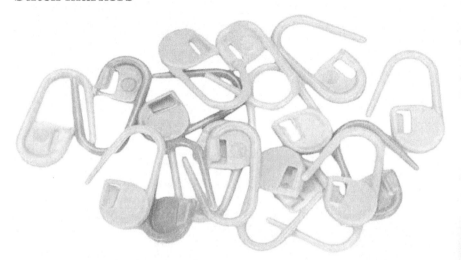

If you're creating amigurumi or a stuffed animal, stitch markers are a must-have. You'll need them to mark where a certain stitch should be located, or how many stitches there are in a specific row. They're available in a range of shapes and sizes, from small safety pins to a large plastic tag that can be threaded through the corresponding stitch for marking purposes.

Garment cheat sheets

If you are working on garments, you'll also need a couple of cheat sheets for your pattern. They're helpful to have for measuring your gauge, and they'll help you make sure that you're crocheting to the size of the pattern.

Digital row counters

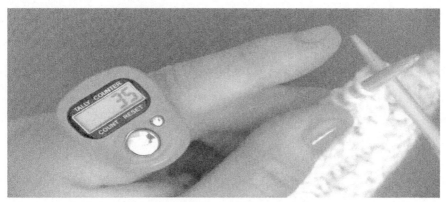

This is an amazing little tool that can be very useful for keeping track of your rows, especially if you are crocheting a lot of large projects. The digital counters are so easy to use - all you need to do is put it on your finger (with an adjustable strap) and press the button to count your rows. Then, when you've finished and put the project away, just tap it to reset your numbers!

The only drawback to this is that they're usually pretty expensive, but it's worth investing in one if you are serious about your crocheting!

Yarn bowls

If your yarn gets tangled when you are working on your crochet project, then a yarn bowl is the answer. These are handy because they have a slit where the yarn can flow through, and they also have a resting spot for your skein so it doesn't get tangled when you're not looking!

Scissors

You'll want a pair of sharp scissors to cut your yarn. There are a wide variety of scissors that can be used for crochet, but a good pair will be sharp and easy to handle.

Foldable scissors are a good option, as they fold up into a compact shape that's easy to pack when not in use. They're a great choice for travel and are a must-have in any crafter's toolbox!

Understanding Common Crochet Terms

When you're just starting to crochet, it can be easy to get confused by the terms used in patterns. The best way to avoid this is to familiarize yourself with the common crochet terms that are commonly used. This can be a great way to ensure that you're following the pattern correctly and saving yourself time in the long run!

-Ch-CH (Crochet chain) This is the most common crochet term, as you'll see nearly all patterns begin with chains. However, it's important to note that ch is only one of several types of stitches that are used in crocheting.

C-CL (Cluster)

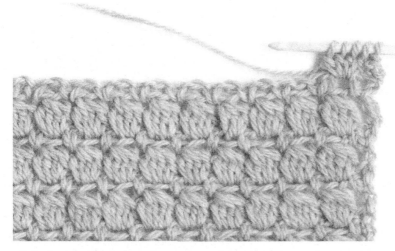

This is another crochet term that you'll see in many patterns, as it refers to cluster stitches, which are groups of stitches worked together to form a pattern. There are several different types of cluster stitches, so be sure to read your pattern carefully to ensure you understand what they mean.

-Dc(double crochet)

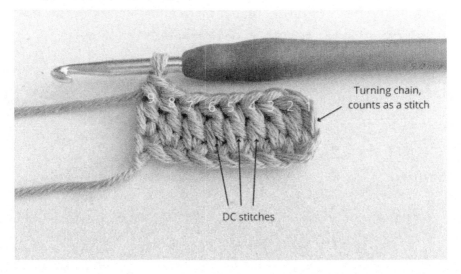

Turning chain, counts as a stitch

DC stitches

This stitch is one of the basic stitches in crocheting and is used to create fabric. It is often used in large projects to add texture and dimension, but can also be used as a regular stitch in smaller projects.

-Hdc(half double crochet)

This crochet stitch is in between the single and double crochet stitches in height. It's a standard stitch for basic crochet projects and is the basis of most crochet blankets.

-Tr-CH (Treble crochet)

This is another common crochet term, as it is one of the taller basic stitches in crocheting. It's a great option for larger projects that need to be worked in taller vertical bars.

-Bp-CH (Back post crochet)

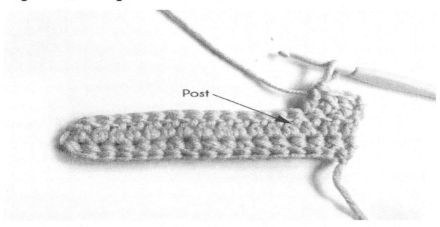

This stitch is a variation of the double crochet and is a great option for larger projects that need a higher crocheting height. It is a great choice for crocheting hats or other large items that need to be a little more secure.

-Tp-CH (turning post crochet)

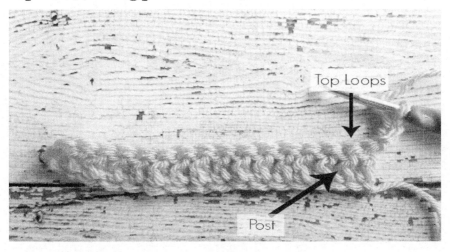

This stitches is used in some crochet projects to turn your work and increase the height of the finished product. It is a great way to increase the height of your project without having to work extra stitches into each row, which can be tedious.

-Tw-CH (treble crochet)

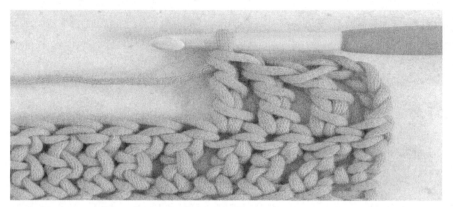

This is one of the taller basic stitches in Crochet, and it's a great option for larger projects such as blankets that require a lot of stitching. It's a great option if you want to use the same yarn throughout your project, but in a different color than what you're working with.

-Bb-CH (bobble)

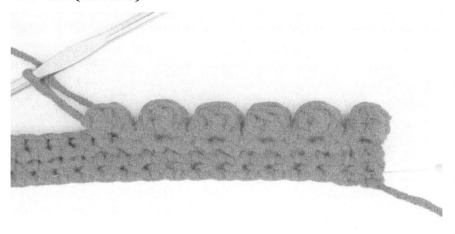

It's a variation of the dc3tog and dc5tog stitches that are worked half way into the next stitch.

-Bb-CL (bobble)

This is a crochet stitch that is often worked in the same way as the dc3tog or dc5tog stitches, but is not a decrease. These are sometimes used to bump out the front of a design, but they are not always followed by a single crochet that makes them look like a bobble.

How to Hold the Crochet Hook

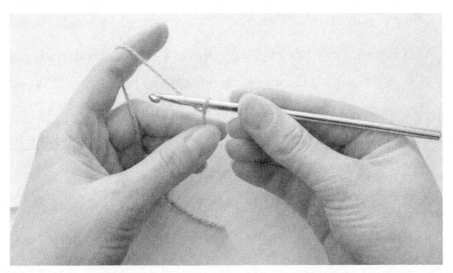

When you hold the crochet hook, it is important to find a grip that feels right for you. If you are not comfortable, your hand could cramp and your stitches may not be even. It is also important to keep the correct tension as you crochet so that you get the best results from your project.

The Pencil Grip

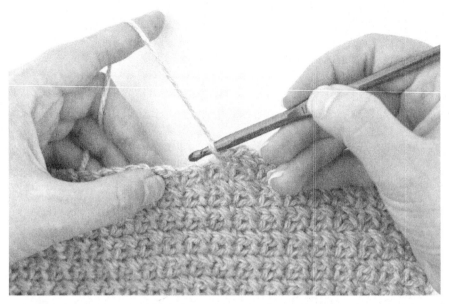

Crocheters who prefer this grip find it easier on their hands because the hook doesn't shift position as they work. It is usually the first grip many crocheters use, but you can always experiment with other holds to find the one that works for you.

The Knife Grip

This grip is a bit more popular than the pencil grip, but it doesn't mean that you have to stick with it if it doesn't feel natural or comfortable for you. You can try holding the hook in the knife position, just as you would a table knife to cut food, and see how it feels for you.

The knife grip is said to be easy on the hands but it isn't as precise as a pencil grip. It is a good grip for large hooks and Tunisian crochet.

It is recommended to learn how to hold the crochet hook before you start working on your project because it's an essential skill for crocheting. You can practice holding the hook while doing a slip knot, making a chain, or a row of single crochet to help you learn how to hold it comfortably.

You can also learn to hold the hook by following a video tutorial or reading a blog post from a skilled crocheter who has used different positions for a while. Once you know how to hold the hook in a way that feels natural and comfortable for you, you will be able to use it for any project!

Another way to hold the crochet hook is by wrapping the ball end of your yarn over the back of your forefinger, then over the middle finger and finally over your index finger. This is a very simple and efficient way to hold the yarn, but it can be a little awkward to get used to.

The Claw Grip

This grip is a little bit more difficult to get used to because it involves a lot of wrist movement and can lead to discomfort. It is the preferred grip for those who aren't able to grasp their crochet hook as easily or with as much control as they would like.

How to Crochet With One Needle?

Crochet is a versatile needlework that allows you to create all kinds of garments, blankets, and even stuffed dolls. It requires only a hook and yarn, which you can choose from a wide variety of colors and fibers. It's a great choice for beginners, as the basics of crochet are simple and can be learned quickly.

The first step in crocheting is learning how to use the hook. Once you know the basic loops and how to crochet a chain stitch, you can start making more complex projects.

To make a crochet chain stitch, simply wrap the yarn around the hook and pull through to form a loop. This can be done multiple times to make a long chain.

This can be useful when working a large project or if you want to create a thicker fabric. The extra weight will help you keep your stitches in place and give your work a sturdy construction.

You can also use the chain stitch to make a turning chain, which is helpful when you're changing directions with your work. When you're working the second row of single crochet, for example, you'll want to turn the work counterclockwise so that you can work across the tops of the stitches from the previous row.

If you're working a pattern with repeating rows or patterns, it can be a good idea to use a stitch marker. Stitch markers are particularly useful if you're planning on leaving your project unfinished for a while, as they'll keep track of the rows or stitches that you've already completed and prevent them from coming loose. They're often sold in sets of several, so you can have them on hand for different projects.

A small pair of scissors is always handy for snipping the ends of your yarn, as you'll need to do this when you're finishing your project or when you're starting a new one. You can also find special yarn snippers that will cut through yarn with ease and won't snag the stitches or pull on your yarn.

You'll want to select the yarn for your project with care, especially if you're a beginner. It should be a medium-weight, durable yarn that is easy to work with and doesn't bleed when it's wet. It's best to begin with a smooth, soft-textured yarn (like a cotton blend) as you're first learning to crochet. Learn them all, and you'll be well on your way to creating beautiful, textured projects!

Choosing the Right Yarn for Your Project

You can use a range of yarns, including wool, cotton, acrylic, and even silk blends.

Chapter 2: How To Read A Crochet Pattern?

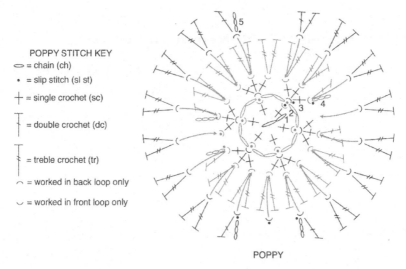

POPPY STITCH KEY
- ⊃ = chain (ch)
- • = slip stitch (sl st)
- + = single crochet (sc)
- ⊺ = double crochet (dc)
- ⨦ = treble crochet (tr)
- ⌢ = worked in back loop only
- ⌣ = worked in front loop only

POPPY

Reading a crochet pattern can be intimidating, especially for beginners. But don't worry, you're not alone! As with any new skill, the learning curve is gradual and takes time. Once you've mastered the basic skills, however, reading patterns isn't nearly as difficult as it first seems!

Getting Started

As you start to look at crochet patterns, the first things you'll notice are headings and sections that contain all sorts of useful information. These often include yarn, stitch, measurement and gauge information. It's easy to skip over these and not take the time to read them, but these can be critical pieces of information that will save you from hours of frustration or a ruined garment!

Yarn Terms & Special Stitches

As a crocheter, you'll often come across crochet terms that are used in different ways in different parts of the world. Thankfully, most of the terms you'll encounter on crochet patterns are universal and can be learned in just a few days.

Crochet Terms You'll Need to Know

There are a few common crochet terms you'll need to learn in order to understand the written instructions on your crochet pattern. These are all important to know because they'll help you to avoid confusion when working the pattern.

Symbols

Having the ability to read crochet symbols will help you to expand your options when working with different types of patterns. Most crochet charts use a set of standard crochet symbols, which you can find in a key that's included with the pattern or on the pattern page itself.

These symbols are a great way to simplify complicated stitch patterns and make them easier for beginner crocheters to follow. If you're new to reading crochet, try working with a simple pattern to help you get the hang of the symbols and make sure you're saying them aloud in a crochet language that makes sense.

Parentheses / Asterisks / Brackets

Repeat symbols can be a bit confusing, but they're important to know so you can follow a pattern accurately and easily. These repeat symbols are usually written inside parentheses, asterisks or brackets, and they tell you when to work the next part of the pattern repeat.

Once you know the meaning of each crochet symbol, you'll be able to read and follow any crochet pattern without too much trouble. Just remember to break long sections of instruction into bullets so you can read each part in turn and not miss any steps along the way!

How to Read a Crochet Pattern

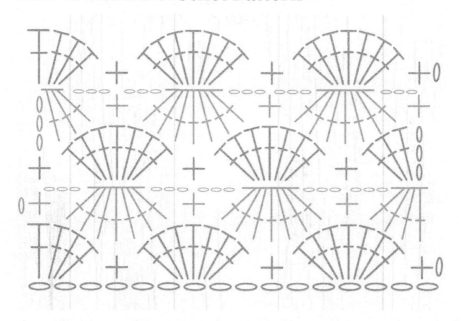

You will also need to be familiar with stitch abbreviations, which are shorthands that indicate a set of instructions in the most concise way possible.

Stitches and abbreviations are written in both English and US terminology, so you need to make sure that the pattern you choose is aimed at the skill level you are most comfortable with. If you are completely new to crochet, start with patterns aimed at beginners and work your way up from there.

Symbols and abbreviations are usually found in the crochet stitch guide, which is a section of the pattern that describes the various stitches used in the project. They are used to help you visualize the stitches and understand what they are going to look like when you complete the project.

Chain spaces are another common crochet term that you will see in a crochet pattern. A chain space is a space created by chaining and skipping stitches.

You will also find symbols in a crochet pattern that tell you how many stitches are in each row or round. These symbols can be parentheses, brackets or asterisks. They are used to communicate how many stitches are in each stitch or row, or how many chains are required for a particular size.

Charts are often included with a crochet pattern and can be a great way to visualize the stitches. They are typically full of symbols arranged in such a way that it basically shows you the whole pattern.

There are some really great patterns out there that come with their own charts that can be a big help. These charts show you exactly how the stitch you are crocheting will fit together.

They are also a great way to see what the finished project will look like before you begin. This can save you hours of frustration because you will know what to expect and not have to figure it out as you go along.

This can be particularly helpful if you are making a garment and the pattern calls for a gauge swatch. You will want to check your gauge before you begin and make sure that you are using the proper hook size. This will prevent you from having to rip out your project because it is too large or too small.

Learning to read a crochet pattern isn't hard, but it does take practice. It is a good idea to go slowly - even slower than you think is needed - so that you don't get frustrated with yourself. By taking your time, you can become an expert at reading a crochet pattern and will soon be able to tackle complicated projects!

How Symbols Can Help Tell Your Story

Symbols are an essential part of storytelling, and there are many ways that they can help you tell your story. They can show rather than tell, connect themes and make your writing more vivid and meaningful without overtaking the narrative with unnecessary detail.

The first step in learning about symbols is to become familiar with the different types of symbolism that are used throughout literature and visual design. This can be done through reading, or simply observing the symbols that are used in your own work.

Use a Style to Reference Symbols

When you are using symbol styles in ArcGIS, you can reference those that you use frequently to save you time searching for symbols. The contents of your referenced styles appear in the Symbol Selector dialog boxes for easy access.

You can also search for symbols by name or keyword. This way, you can easily find the ones that are most relevant to your project.

Embrace The Past

Some symbols, such as the dove, have a rich history and are associated with peace, tranquility and grace. They are commonly used to convey this message, both in religious ceremonies and for communication purposes.

They can be found in a variety of shapes and sizes. For example, the crescent is a popular symbol for Islam. This symbol has a symmetrical shape and is often paired with the morning star, which represents femininity and balance.

Another common symbol is the moon, which is associated with femininity, fertility and the rhythm of time. It is used in a variety of rituals, including wedding ceremonies and funerals.

The color blue symbolizes calmness and melancholy, but it can also be a symbol for hope and new growth. It is a color that is commonly associated with love and romance, but it can also be used to signify danger.

Symbols are a great way to illustrate emotion, as well as provide a visual aid for emotional regulation strategies. In addition, they can be a tool to show how your characters and objects can respond in different ways to a particular situation.

Consider a Coat of Arms to Create a Historic Identity

A coat of arms is an ancient symbol that has been adopted by many brands to help them cultivate a sense of heritage and tradition. Originally used to identify the owners of specific territories and trade routes, these ancient symbols are a great way for designers to express their brand in a more traditional manner.

In addition, a coat of arms can be an effective way to establish a brand's uniqueness by combining modern and ancient elements. In fact, many designers today are repurposing medieval heraldry for modern brands and competing factions that are seeking to establish their own sense of place.

Creating and interpreting symbolism can be a daunting task, but it is well worth the effort. As with all aspects of writing, the more you know about symbolism and how it can be used, the more effective your literary work will be.

Levels Of Skill

Skill levels are a way of assessing how well you perform a job. This information can be used by employers to determine whether you are a good candidate for a position and if so, how quickly you should be promoted.

The level of skill that you possess reflects the amount of expertise that you have in a particular area. Generally, the higher the level of skill that you have in an area, the better the job opportunity that you can be considered for.

There are three levels of skill: Entry, Fully Effective, and Mastery. Each of these reflects a different standard of proficiency that is expected by the employer.

Entry - Staff who are new to a position may display this proficiency, as it is the minimum expected of staff in that role. They are usually expected to move through this level fairly quickly and are likely to be sought out by other staff for advice or help.

Fully Effective - Staff who have demonstrated full proficiency in their role can be trusted to deliver the results that are needed by the employer. They often show that they are able to handle complex situations and are likely to be called upon for guidance or assistance when necessary.

Masters - Staff who have mastered their role can be trusted to provide the most accurate and practical advice to others. They will often be asked to explain complicated scenarios and can present practical solutions or process improvements that relate to their competency areas.

These staff will usually be highly regarded and sought after by the employer. They can be a key factor in the success of the organisation and should be recognized for their contribution.

The level of skill you have should also be reflected in the experience section of your resume. This should be the place where you describe how you have used specific skills in the past and what examples you can give to demonstrate your abilities.

A good place to start is by focusing on the technical skills that you have to offer and which are directly related to your job duties. This will ensure that you can easily be distinguished from other candidates who don't have the same types of skills.

You can also include your soft skills, such as communication, if they are important to the position you are applying for. These can be difficult to quantify with a skill level, but they can be reflected in the experience section of your profile.

In order to understand which skill levels to assign, it is a good idea to review the job description that you are applying for. Taking this into account will ensure that you can accurately reflect your skill levels in the resume.

There are several ways to organize the skills you have to offer in your CV, but one of the most effective methods is to categorize them by their level of proficiency and to indicate your experience level on the right hand side of each skill. This will help to differentiate the skills that are more directly applicable to a specific job and those which are more related to your personality and work ethic.

Details Of The Pattern

A pattern is a set of information that relates to a specific subject. It can be in the form of a list, description, or other format. A pattern is most often used to organize and present information about a topic.

Classification design patterns arrange similar items into classes or categories. These classifications can be very useful when analyzing data or other information.

When you're writing a paper or article about something, you might use a classification pattern to present the information in a way that helps your audience understand and categorize the material. This type of pattern is especially effective when you're trying to convey the idea that certain kinds of things are more similar than others.

For example, if you're writing an article about a certain kind of stringed instrument or a sport that uses balls, you might use a classification pattern that groups these things into different "types" so that your reader can easily find what they're looking for.

A classification pattern can also be applied to other types of data, such as stock prices. When you're analyzing stocks, you might want to show how many days prices have been rising before each peak. A pattern that lists the peaks and the number of days before each one can help your readers see this relationship clearly.

The pattern that you select for this purpose should be a topical pattern. This is the most commonly used pattern format, and will generally work well when other patterns do not.

This type of pattern is effective when you want to organize your information by dividing it into different sections, such as causes and effects. This is especially useful when you're writing a persuasive piece of work that persuades your readers to take action.

Master-detail designs are a popular style of layout for web pages and apps. They make use of a small amount of horizontal space to provide a lot of detail without having to scroll. These designs are also easy to adapt for various display sizes and screen orientations.

In order to create this type of layout, you must first determine what type of content you want to display. For example, if you're creating an app that requires a user to sign up for a subscription service, then the app should display information about the service.

Then you can decide how to layout that content on the screen. For example, if you need to display the name of the service and the date when it was first available, you can use a stacked bar chart or a column-based grid.

You can also use this type of layout when you need to display a large amount of information, such as a long list of products. This type of layout can be very useful when you're designing a database or other data-intensive application.

This can be helpful when you're trying to persuade someone to do something or when you want to highlight the significance of a particular event in history.

How to Properly Use Abbreviations when crotcheting

When crocheting, abbreviations are used to make patterns easier to read and follow. Here are some tips to help you properly use abbreviations in crochet patterns:

Familiarize yourself with common abbreviations: Before you start working on a pattern, familiarize yourself with the most commonly used abbreviations in crochet patterns, such as sc (single crochet), dc (double crochet), hdc (half double crochet), etc.

Use a standardized list of abbreviations: Make sure to use a standardized list of abbreviations, such as those provided by the Craft Yarn Council. This will ensure that the pattern is consistent and easy to follow.

Clearly define abbreviations: If a pattern uses an uncommon or unique abbreviation, make sure to clearly define it in the pattern. This will prevent confusion and ensure that the pattern is followed correctly.

Use abbreviations consistently: Once you have defined the abbreviations you will use in the pattern, make sure to use them consistently throughout. This will make the pattern easy to follow and prevent confusion.

Pay attention to context: Make sure to pay attention to the context in which the abbreviation is used. For example, if the abbreviation is used in the instructions for a stitch, make sure to follow the instructions carefully to ensure the stitch is made correctly.

By following these tips, you can ensure that you use abbreviations correctly and effectively when crocheting.

Look At The Stitches And Abbreviations Used In The Pattern

This is a great way to learn how to read a pattern quickly and effectively, and it'll also help you memorize the pattern's instructions so that you don't get confused when you're trying to follow it.

There are several basic stitch types you'll find in most crochet patterns, including chains, single crochet, and double crochet. Most of these terms are easy to remember, and they'll become a familiar part of your crochet vocabulary soon after you start reading a pattern.

Ch(s) means chain, and this is one of the most common abbreviations you'll see. Crochet patterns often include chains throughout their designs, and as a beginner crocheter you'll probably want to know what these are so that you can easily work them into your finished project.

Cl (cluster) is another term you'll encounter when reading a crochet pattern, and it refers to clusters of stitches. There are several different kinds of cluster stitches, so it's best to read the pattern carefully to make sure you understand what type you're working into your project.

Dc (double crochet) is a very popular basic stitch, and one of the most widely used by crocheters. This is a basic crochet stitch that's taller than the standard single crochet, and it's often found in sweaters and other projects where a more pronounced crochet design is necessary.

Tr (treble) is another basic crochet stitch, and it's also a common one in patterns. This is a slightly taller crochet stitch than the standard treble, and it's often found in sweaters, baby clothes, and other projects where a more pronounced design is necessary.

Inc (increase) is another technique that's often used in shaping, just like decreasing (dec). This is a very easy crochet technique to master, and you'll see it a lot in patterns.

FP (front post) is another term that's commonly used in crochet patterns, and it's a bit taller than the BL (back loop) and BLO (back loop only) terms mentioned above.

Pc (popcorn) is a stitch that's sometimes used to create a little bump along the edge of lacy items. It's a simple stitch to do, and it's often found in patterns that feature textured stitches such as popcorns.

UFO (unfinished object) is another common term in crochet patterns, and it's essentially an unfinished crochet project that's been set aside. It's a great place to keep track of your progress, and it's often referred to in written conversation between crocheters.

WS (wrong side) is an important term in the beginning row of a pattern, and it's a good idea to pay close attention to this, since it can be crucial when joining pieces together. This is especially true if the piece you're working on is made in more than one piece, and the pattern wants to be facing outwards.

Many crochet patterns will also have their own special stitches, which are usually described at the beginning of a pattern near gauge information. These stitches are a great way to add personality and detail to a garment, so it's important to pay close attention to the pattern instructions when learning how to make them.

Tips And Tricks For Reading A Crochet Pattern

If you're new to crocheting, reading patterns can be daunting. But it doesn't have to be a complicated or confusing process, and with a few tips, you'll be able to decipher the instructions on any pattern in no time at all!

Stitches And Abbreviations

Crochet patterns rely on specific punctuation to indicate repeats of stitches, sections and entire rows. These symbols include asterisks, semicolons and parentheses, as well as brackets.

Stitches are the basic units of a crochet project, and it's important to know what they are before you start your craft. This will help you understand the patterns better and make your projects easier to follow.

A stitch is basically a loop on the yarn that you pull through your hook to form the shape of the project. It varies in size depending on the type of stitch and how much yarn you're using, so it's important to pay attention to the specific terms of each stitch as they appear in a crochet pattern.

In addition to written instructions, some crochet patterns will also include a chart or image that is meant to enhance your understanding of the pattern. It can be a great way to make a complicated pattern easier to read, especially for visual learners.

This section usually contains notes from the designer on topics like the style of writing the pattern, any tutorials they have included and anything that they think you may need to know before you begin your project.

It can also include links to other useful websites or blogs where you can find more information on the subject. Some patterns even include links to YouTube videos that show you how to complete the pattern in a step-by-step fashion!

The Stitches And Abbreviations That Aren't Listed In This Section

A pattern will sometimes list special stitches that are not usually found in other parts of the pattern. These special stitches can vary a lot from pattern to pattern so it's important to always follow the instructions for forming them.

They can often be very tricky to understand at first, so it's a good idea to read the stitch guide carefully and learn how to properly form each one before you start working on your crochet project.

These stitches are most often used for creating garments, but they can also be used for other types of crochet projects such as toys and blankets. They are a great way to try out different techniques and get the feel of how they work before you commit to a full-size project.

Increases And Decreases

In crochet, increases and decreases are a very common way to change the shape of a project. Most patterns will include instructions for a simple increase or decrease at the beginning and end of a round. They can also be used to alter the size of a project by adding or subtracting stitches as required.

You should only use these increases or decreases if they're necessary for the specific pattern. If they aren't, you'll run into a tangle that's difficult to unravel and your project will not turn out as intended.

How to Understand a Crochet Pattern in Another Language

Reading crochet patterns can be confusing at first, but once you understand the basic terms and symbols you'll find that it doesn't take long to get the hang of reading a pattern in another language.

Stitch Abbreviations and Crochet Symbols

The terms and symbols that are used in a crochet pattern make it easy to understand how the stitches work together. For example, a "sc" means single crochet and an "x" or an "+" symbolizes the same stitch. These symbols are simple to memorize and will save you a lot of time in the future, so it's important that you get comfortable with them quickly!

Symbol Charts Explained

A crochet chart is a visual representation of a pattern that combines different symbols to create a drawing of how the different stitches are worked together. You'll have to get used to seeing these symbols, but once you do they'll be just as obvious as the written crochet abbreviations you see in your patterns.

Symbol Charts Explained

The Craft Yarn Council has developed standardized crochet symbols that are used across all types of patterns. These symbols are designed to look like crude representations of stitches, but once you get used to them, they'll be as easy to recognize as the written crochet abbreviations in your patterns.

Symbol Charts are a great way to help you learn how to read a crochet pattern in a new language!

When you're new to reading a crochet pattern, it can be helpful to start with a simple project that doesn't have many instructions. Try making a granny square or even a hat, and once you've finished it, look at the chart that is included in the pattern.

Once you've gotten the hang of reading a crochet chart, it's time to move on to more complex patterns that include multiple stitches and variations of those stitches. These are often called special stitches and they may not be written out fully in the pattern, or they'll be explained in a glossary at the beginning of the pattern.

Notes

The notes section of a crochet pattern is an extra section that may be added to the pattern by the designer. Occasionally these notes will mention something that wasn't said in other sections, and they might also contain links to helpful tutorial videos or blog posts that will help you navigate the pattern.

Usually these extra sections are not necessary, but it's always nice to have some handy advice for when you run into a challenge while working a particular stitch.

Headings & Titles

A pattern often has titles and headings that help you keep track of where the pattern is going. This is especially important when you're working on a large project and want to make sure you're not missing anything along the way.

When reading a crochet pattern, it's important to read each section carefully and thoroughly. This will ensure that you don't miss anything and will allow you to complete the project successfully.

Chapter 3: Basic Crochet Methods

Whether you're crocheting a sweater, baby blanket, or even a scarf, the basic stitches of crochet are essential for creating your project. These crochet stitches are what make your work unique and special, so it's important to know them well.

Chain Stitch (ch) and Slip Knot

The simplest of all crochet techniques, the chain stitch is made by wrapping the yarn around the hook from back to front, catching it in the loop and pulling it through. Repeat this action to create a chain loop that will form the foundation for most of your crochet projects. This chain can be worked in rows or rounds, but is most often used as a turning chain at the beginning of new rows or rounds of crochet.

Double Crochet (dc) and Half-Double Crochet (hdc)

The double crochet is a staple of beginner crocheters because it's very easy to master and makes great projects like baby blankets and scarves. It's also popular in advanced techniques because it's a great way to build height into your project while still allowing for a smooth, even fabric.

This is a basic crochet technique that is used in amigurumi (crocheted dolls or toys) and hats. The dc stitch is also used in many other crochet patterns and is the basis for many crochet designs.

Single Crochet (sc) and Shell Stitch

The single crochet stitch is a very common and versatile stitch. It's easy to learn and works beautifully in both solid and variegated yarns and is especially useful for joining rounds. This stitch can be used to create a variety of shapes and textures, including granny squares and Tunisian stitches.

Another of the crochet basics is the shell stitch, which is commonly used in lacework and colorwork. It can also be used to form a decorative hem or to embellish a project by working it across multiple stitches.

You can use a different color of yarn to create these shells, which will add an extra dimension to the stitch and the finished project. If you're a more advanced crocheter, it's also possible to work these stitches in a treble or double stitch pattern for added texture and depth.

Alternatively, you can try working this stitch using a thinner weight of yarn for a lighter and more airy result. For example, you can work a dc in a light weight cotton yarn to create a very soft, lightweight fabric for baby blankets or scarves.

The shell stitch is one of the most versatile crochet stitches because it can be worked in a variety of ways to form a variety of interesting stitches. For instance, a shell stitch can be worked in an alternating pattern of single crochet and chains to create the moss stitch or a dc and hdc pattern to create the lemon peel stitch.

The Single Crochet Stitch

The Single Crochet Stitch is one of the most basic crochet stitches, and also one of the most versatile. This stitch can be used to create items such as scarves and blankets, and it is very easy to learn.

The stitch is also very practical, since it joins the chain stitches that are often used to make the beginnings of a pattern. You can use this stitch in a variety of ways to increase and decrease the number of stitches on your work, making it very useful for shaping.

To start off, make a swatch to practice your new stitches and techniques. The swatch should be about 4 inches wide and about 9" long.

Starting your swatch: Step 1 (Left): Make a foundation chain of 11 stitches, with the working yarn in front of the work.

Step 2: Turn your work counter-clockwise so that the loops on the wrong side of the swatch are facing you.

Once your work is turned, insert your hook from back to front into the first stitch, right under the top two loops of the "V" that you see on the wrong side. Pull the yarn through both of the V-shaped loops, and a stitch has been made.

Next, repeat this same step in each of the remaining chains. Continue until you have 15 stitches on the right side of your swatch.

Finishing the row: Using the same st as you started with, make a single crochet in each of the remaining single crochets on the right side of your swatch, and finish off by inserting your hook into the next chain stitch.

A very common variation of the single crochet is to use the stitch in the front loop only (FLO), or the back loop only (BLO). This technique creates a ribbed effect that makes it more stretchy as a finished fabric.

Another variation of the single crochet is to make it into a slip knot before you insert your hook into the next stitch. This is very useful when working taller crochet stitches, such as the half-double crochet, and it allows you to avoid any twists in your chain.

Counting your stitches: It's important to count your stitches at the end of each row so you know where you are in your pattern. This will help you to know if you are on track or need to go back and do more work.

When you are learning to crochet, it is important to make sure you have the basics down before you get too advanced and start trying out more complex stitches and techniques. By practicing the single crochet, you'll be able to work more complicated stitches with greater ease in the future.

To practice the single crochet, you can make a quick swatch in worsted weight yarn with a 4mm crochet hook. You can even make a sampler with different types of stitch patterns for fun and experimentation!

The Double Crochet Stich

The Double Crochet Stich (DC) is one of the most basic crochet stitches and is used in a wide variety of patterns. This stitch is roughly twice the height of a single crochet and is ideal for creating a fabric that is fairly solid but not stiff. It looks great in blankets, shawls, afghans, placemats and other home decor items.

Linked Double Crochet

The linked double crochet is a variation on the standard double crochet that creates a more solid and dense result. This stitch eliminates the gaps and holes that you can sometimes see when working a traditional double crochet.

You can also change the yarn type that you use to work this stitch. Cotton and other natural fibers look beautiful when paired with this stitch, but you can also use acrylic, wool or any other type of yarn that you like.

This stitch is a great choice for beginner crocheters and for those who want to practice this important stitch before making larger projects. It is easy to make and works up quickly, so you can easily learn this stitch and start using it to make your favorite items.

Once you have mastered this stitch, try a few of the other basic crochet stitches. Once you master these, you'll be able to confidently move on to the more advanced stitches and techniques in the world of crochet.

Another variation of the double crochet is the half double crochet, or HDC. This stitch is a little less intimidating than the standard double crochet and will help you to get started in this very important stitch.

It is a very popular stitch and works up quickly to create cute baby blankets, cardigans, and other garments for little ones. You can also use this stitch in a variety of other projects for children and adults, such as hats, scarves, socks, and more.

How to Do a Chain Stitch

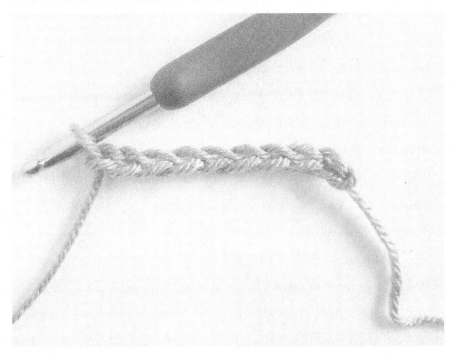

Chain Stitch is one of the most basic and fundamental embroidery stitches that you should know! It is a looped stitch that can be worked on straight or curved lines, and it works very well as an outline stitch or for filling in spaces.

It is a common stitch used in many hand embroidery patterns and has been around for centuries!

How to do a Chain Stitch

To start, take the needle up through the back of your fabric to the front at the beginning of the line to be worked. Bring it up about a stitch length away from the end of the first loop, then insert it under the first loop and take it down near where it came up; do not pull through yet.

Next, wrap the working thread in front of your needle and make a complete turn. The working thread should now form a tight loop that wraps around the needle once. Repeat until the whole stitch has been completed.

If you run out of thread, do not tie off the thread; instead, go back down through the hole where it came up and weave it underneath the existing loops to make an anchoring stitch in the last loop. If this does not work, tug the tail of the first thread until it reduces in size to the same size as the existing loops.

Step 4: Add a Link

To make the next link in your chain, insert your needle through the same hole as the first "anchor" stitch. Pass the thread underneath both threads in that "link." Then, re-insert your needle through the same hole where you made the original "anchor" stitch and pull all the way through (left photo).

Once your chain stitch has a couple of "links," it is time to do some work on your hoop. This is a simple technique that will help you keep your stitches looking great while creating the heavy chain stitch you've been wanting!

You can also use the reversed chain stitch to create some fun and unique effects. This is a technique that will require some trial and error to learn, but you'll be surprised at how much it can add to your stitching!

The reversed chain stitch looks more like a twisted chain, but is actually easier to work than the basic technique. The method is slightly different than the basic chain stitch, but it's easy to understand and will help you master this type of embroidery.

This is an excellent stitch to work in a hoop, as it can be very difficult to get the right amount of tension when you're hand-stitching. This stitch is perfect for beginners, because it's easy to see what you're doing and the strands of floss won't separate or get tangled.

How to Work a Slip Stitch

The slip stitch is a basic crochet stitch that can be used to shape, decorate and join rounds. It also has a variety of uses in other areas of the craft.

It is often used to join round stitches in a granny square, or to travel from one part of a project to another without producing any visible stitches. It can also be used for shaping armholes and other details of sweaters or hats.

To work a slip stitch, make a chain of the desired length (if using a crochet hook), insert your hook into the last stitch of the foundation chain, yarn over and draw the yarn through the loop on your hook in one motion.

Depending on the pattern, you may be asked to work the slip stitch purlwise or knitwise. The main thing to remember is that both are good ways to do it, but purlwise tends to be a bit easier, so it's worth trying this technique!

You might also be asked to use this stitch to "sew" smaller pieces of crochet together, like granny squares for a blanket or panels for a sweater. To do this, simply put your hook through the two edges of your work, yarn over and pull all the loops through in one movement.

It's important to keep your tension even when working a slip stitch, or else the fabric can pucker. This is especially true if you're working slip-stitch colourwork patterns, where floats (lines of spare yarn) are commonplace.

If you're not careful, you can end up with a large number of floats. This can look a little unsightly, so it's a good idea to keep them all evenly spaced out and not pull on them too tightly.

Floats are a great decorative element for shawls and wraps, but they can be a pain to work! The good news is that if you're not too keen on them, there are many other techniques to use instead.

You can also use a slip stitch to "sew" a hem or attach binding inside an armhole. These techniques are a lot easier than topstitching, and you can do them in any fabric or stitch.

You can use a slip stitch to sew a button closure onto a garment, too. This is a great technique to use when you want the button closure to be concealed under the hem or inside the armhole, so that it doesn't show up on the outside of the item.

How to Work Half Double Crochet

Half Double Crochet (or HDC) is a great stitch for crocheting hats, sweaters, scarves and baby blankets. It creates a warm, cozy fabric without the holes and gaps that bigger stitches can make.

A Half Double Crochet Stitch Explained

One of the best things about a half double crochet stitch is that it can be used in a variety of projects and is easy to master. You can learn to half double crochet with any yarn and crochet hook you have, and there are no hard-and-fast rules as to which size of hook or weight of yarn is best for the stitch.

There are many different ways to work a half double crochet, and you can even use this stitch in the round as well. This is known as a hdc in the third loop, and it can add a ridge to your work that looks a bit like a raised chain stitch.

To start your first row of half double crochet, you need to create a turning chain.

You can use any number of chain stitches for your turning chain. However, most experts recommend working two turning chains to give your stitches enough room to move around while you are creating your project.

Next, work your first hdc into the top of the first chain that you made to create your turning chain. Repeat this step until you have worked your first hdc into the tops of all of the chains that you have created.

Then, turn your work over so that you are looking at the back of the work. This will allow you to continue working your hdc stitches on the other side of the chain that you started with.

Now, follow the same steps for each half double crochet in the row until you have finished the entire row of hdc. You can also repeat the above steps for a second row, but you will not need to create a turning chain at the end of the second row.

Step 4: Yarn Over Again

In this final step, you will pull the yarn through three loops on the hook, which is the same as a single crochet. But instead of drawing up a single loop, you will draw up a third loop, which is the special loop that you created when you made your first half double crochet.

Depending on how you want the final project to look, you may or may not count this as a half double crochet stitch. Some designers prefer to have the turning chain not count as a stitch, while others want it to count as a hdc stitch. The choice is yours, but it does help to practice with a swatch to figure out which way you prefer to do it.

Chapter 4: Quick And Easy Beginner Crochet Patterns

Crochet is an easy craft to learn, with just a few basic stitches to start making a wide range of projects. With the right crochet tools and the perfect beginner crochet patterns, you can start crafting with confidence!

Whether you want to make something for yourself or give it as a gift, there are tons of beginner-friendly patterns to choose from. From simple blankets to cozy hats and scarves, there's something for everyone!

Some of these projects are quick and easy to make, while others take a bit more time. Whatever your style, these beginner-friendly crochet patterns will have you crocheting up something beautiful in no time!

These free patterns are great for beginners, and they're sure to give you the skills you need to get started with crocheting. They'll also help you practice new crochet techniques, so you can learn to master more advanced stitches and become a more skilled crocheter in no time!

Headbands are always a fun way to add a touch of whimsy to your wardrobe. These free crochet patterns for a bobble headband are the perfect way to do just that!

You can even crochet them in different colors to match your outfits. And they're also great for keeping your ears warm in the winter!

This crochet pattern is perfect for a newbie because it requires just a single skein of yarn and some basic crochet stitches. The pattern is easy to follow, and the result is a cute and stylish headband that's sure to please.

Another quick and easy project is this cute mug warmer. You can make it in a variety of colors and it's sure to be a hit with friends and family. This is the perfect beginner crochet project for someone who wants to try out a new skill, and it's also a nice project for the whole family to do together!

Baskets are a great beginner-friendly project. These are easy to crochet and are a great way to carry your yarn and hooks with you!

This woven basket is the perfect size for carrying your crochet hooks and other small items. The striped pattern is easy to work with, and it's a great beginner-friendly project for anyone who's new to crocheting.

These amigurumi balls are adorable and easy to make! You just need some Worsted Weight Yarn, a 3.5 mm crochet hook, safety eyes, Poly-fil, and a needle!

Using just these four beginner-friendly patterns, you'll be able to start your crochet journey with confidence! And the best part? Once you're ready to move on to more advanced projects, there are plenty of other free patterns that can help you get the hang of a new skill!

Use a Slip Stitch to Start Your Projects

All crochet projects begin with the slip stitch, which is created by placing your hook through the front of your work. This allows your stitches to be separated by a gap, which creates a feminine feel and helps the fabric to drape better.

How to Make a Crochet Scarf

A Crochet Scarf is a perfect way to add a touch of warmth to your outfit. It's also a great way to add color and texture, making it a beautiful accessory for all seasons.

Embroider Your Crochet Scarf

You can embellish the scarf with a variety of things, including embroidery, tassels, or crochet buttons.

These are all easy to make, and the result is a beautiful accessory that you'll enjoy wearing every day!

The first thing you need to do is swatch your yarn. Swatching helps you determine how long your scarf will be, as well as the number of stitches you will need.

Using the chain stitch, work a single crochet into each chain until you have the desired width of your scarf. Next, you will need to double crochet these chains together. This will give you the bulk of the scarf and keep it from curling up too much, which would look bad.

Repeat this step until you have a few rows of double crochet stitch, or as many as you need to reach the length you want your scarf to be. You should now have a nice, thick scarf that you can wrap around your neck and feel cozy and warm. Some people prefer wools for their ability to withstand the elements, while others may choose an acrylic or silk yarn for their preference in drape and color.

Once you have a selection of yarns, decide on the colors that will go best with your scarf. You can try a few different shades to see which ones will match your favorite outfits the most, or you can stick with just one color and make a simple, plain scarf.

If you have a lot of leftover yarn, consider making a few tassels and adding them to the ends of your scarf. These tassels are super fast and easy to make, so you'll have a finished product in no time at all!

Choosing Your Yarn for a Crochet Scarf

A good crochet yarn can really make or break your project. It should be comfortable, durable, and easy to take care of. You should also think about how you plan on wearing your scarf, as this will affect which yarn will be better for you.

You'll want to use a yarn that has a nice sheen, as it will look very attractive on your finished scarf. A lyocell yarn, such as this one from Stitching Together, has the perfect sheen and will give your crochet scarf a very elegant look.

How to Make a Crochet Beanie

There are so many different ways to wear a crochet beanie.

The Body of the Crochet Beanie is Worked in a Moss Stitch

This easy crochet hat is worked in an extended moss stitch. It is similar to the linen stitch, but it uses a double crochet stitch in place of a single crochet. This gives the hat a slightly different look, but it also works up much faster!

The Ribbed Border is Made from a Single-Skein Yarn

This classic ribbed beanie pattern is made with just one skein of bulky weight yarn. It's perfect for beginners, and it comes together in a snap.

The hat is crafted with an easy-to-remember stitch pattern that resembles knit ribbing, creating a fabric that's textured and stretchy. It's also a great project for advanced crocheters who want to practice a new skill without breaking the bank!

To Start Your Crochet Hat

Using the hook and the main color of your yarn, begin by ch 2 (counts as a sc). Next, dc in each of the next 3 sts. Repeat across until your hat measures approximately 19.5" long. Then seam your hat together using the last row of stitches.

To Alter the Pattern

After making your hat, you'll change up the stitch pattern a bit to increase the size of your hat. This can be done in several different ways depending on the size of your hat.

Round 5: ch 2, *1dc in the next 4 sts, 2dc in the next. Rep from * until the hat has approximately 60 sts, then stop increasing at that point. Alternatively, you can continue to increase until the hat has approximately 72 sts, then stop increasing at the same point.

You can also work your hat in a color-block design to create a stylish ribbed beanie that will look fantastic with any outfit. Just be sure to switch your main color mid-row and complete the row in the other color.

Add Some Slouch

This also helps to increase the overall width of your hat and give it a more slouchy look.

Finish Your Hat With a Pompom

The pom pom on this beanie can be made from either the main yarn or an additional yarn of your choice. It is a fun and festive way to finish your beanie!

Another option is to add a faux fur pom pom. This will give your hat an even more luxurious feel and add extra dimension to the finished product.

You can use any kind of yarn you like to crochet this beanie, but I recommend using a 4-ply worsted weight that's either acrylic or wool. The thicker the yarn, the more elasticity it has and the better its quality will be.

Crochet Kitty Projects For Your Cat

A cat is a wonderful animal to have and crocheting kitty projects can be a great way to add some fun and creativity to your home. From cozy hats to catnip toys, there are so many adorable kitty-themed projects out there that you can make for your favorite feline.

Fish Toy

Your cats love fish and this crocheted toy will give them the opportunity to get their fix. The pattern is really simple and the finished project works up really fast, so you can have it ready for your kitty in no time at all.

Lazy Kitty This is another quick and easy cat crochet pattern that makes a really cute lazy kitty to relax with after a long day of work. The pattern is very simple and only takes a few stitches and about an hour of your time to complete. You can even make a lot of these and keep them around to keep your cat company throughout the day.

T-Shirt Bed This is a great way to reuse old jersey t-shirts and use them to make your own kitty bed. You can find jersey t-shirts at thrift stores for a couple of dollars each and this bed only uses one or two of them.

Crochet Kitten Collar This collar is really comfortable and works up really quickly. It's also much less expensive than the ones you can buy at pet stores.

Bucket Hat This bucket hat is super adorable and it can be made in a variety of colors to match your cats' wardrobe. The hat is also soft and comfy so it's perfect for them to play with.

Catnip Stick This is another fun way to give your cat some catnip, which they'll definitely love. The finished product works up quite quickly and you can fill it with catnip, which is a nice way to reward your kitty for good behavior or just to encourage them to be a bit more active.

Amigurumi This is another really fun and creative way to crochet and this collection includes a wide range of adorable cat amigurumi patterns. They're a lot of fun to make and are sure to bring joy to the ones who receive them.

Stitch Marker This is a helpful tool to use for keeping track of your stitches and making it easier to follow patterns when you're working on multiple projects. It's also useful for helping you to remember where each stitch goes in a given round.

Pusheen If you're a fan of this internet cat, you'll love this crochet pattern to bring her to life! It's a pretty easy pattern and the result will be an adorable little cat that looks just like the colorful, energetic kitty you know and love.

This is a really cute project that would be a great gift for a cat lover or someone who may be getting a new cat. It's also a fun activity to do with friends and family.

Baby Lamb Farm Animal Crochet Pattern

If you're a fan of cute, fluffy animals, then crocheting an amigurumi is right up your alley! These adorable plush toys are a great way to give your friends and family members something special that they can enjoy for years to come. They also make a perfect gift for children of all ages, and can be used as cuddle buddies to help them relax or fall asleep.

Whether you are looking to make a crocheted baby lamb for a newborn or just want to add some fun to your home, there are plenty of amazing crochet animal patterns to choose from. Crochet is a fun and easy hobby that anyone can do, even those who are new to the craft.

There are many different types of animals that can be crocheted, including fish, birds, and other wildlife. These creatures are all very easy to make, and can be made with a range of different yarns and hook sizes.

These patterns are great for introducing crochet to beginners, as they are often fairly simple to follow and include clear instructions. You can also purchase some amigurumi patterns that are more complicated, so that you have a few options to choose from when making an amigurumi animal.

Amigurumi is an art that was first practiced in Japan, but has been popular in the United States in the past few decades. These stuffed creatures are very soft, and can be made in a wide range of sizes and shapes.

They are very popular with kids, and can be found in all kinds of different stores. They're also extremely affordable to make, and are perfect for gifts.

Creating an amigurumi is a great way to express yourself. You can personalize them with a name and a unique design, and they will be sure to bring smiles to your friends and family.

You can also add accessories to these amigurumi toys, like a bow or bell for example, which will make them stand out from the crowd. You can even purchase kits that will contain everything you need to make an amigurumi.

These amigurumi animal patterns are great for people of all skill levels and can be very rewarding to complete. The process of crocheting these amigurumi is not difficult, and once they are done, they will have a very unique appearance that will be loved by everyone who sees them.

If you are not sure where to start with these amigurumi patterns, try using some of these free patterns for inspiration. These free patterns are all incredibly easy to follow, and you'll be sure to have a great time creating your own adorable amigurumi animals.

Having a baby is always a big deal, and what better way to celebrate the birth of your little one than with a handmade gift? These amigurumi patterns are the perfect choice to make your own heirloom-quality baby lamb, and they're easy enough for beginners to follow.

How to Create a Baby Blanket Crochet Pattern

A Baby Blanket Crochet Pattern is the perfect project for a new mom or anyone who wants to make a special gift for a new baby. It is easy to create and can be made in a variety of colors and sizes to fit any baby's needs.

The blanket can be used in a baby's cot, crib, stroller, pram or anywhere else a soft, cozy blanket is needed! The blanket is a great project for beginners because the pattern includes simple stitches that are easy to follow. It is also easy to resize the blanket and adjust the number of repeats.

Choosing the Right Stitch

For a crochet blanket, you want to choose a stitch that is easy to work, looks great and will hold up well with the type of yarn you are using. There are many different types of stitches, so it is important to choose a stitch that fits your design preference and the thickness of the yarn you are using.

A good basic stitch for a blanket is the double crochet (dc) stitch, which creates a close and dense fabric. This type of stitch will work up quickly and can be worked in a variety of colors to add interest.

Another classic crochet stitch is the ripple stitch, which can be used to create a textured blanket in a variety of colors and styles. This type of stitch is often used for afghans but it can be adapted to baby blankets too.

Moss Stitch

The moss stitch, or granite or linen stitch, is a quick and easy way to create a beautiful fabric with great drape. This stitch is a great choice for blankets because it can be worked in a variety of colors and can also be used with self-striping yarn to produce stunning color changes.

Cluster Stitch

The cluster stitch is a popular stitch for blankets because it is easy to work and gives the blanket a soft, cozy look that will be loved by baby. It is also a great project for beginners as it is a very simple stitch that is easier than the double crochet stitch and can be completed in no time at all!

Bobble Stitch

The bobble stitch is a fun and versatile stitch that can be used for a variety of projects including baby blankets. This stitch has a few differences from the regular double crochet stitch that makes it easier for beginners to learn.

Puff Stitch

The puff stitch is another popular stitch for blankets because it is a fast and easy stitch to learn and can be worked in a variety of styles. It is a great project for beginners as it is easy to use and it will give you a blanket that has a unique texture.

Lace Stitch

A lacy crochet stitch is a great option for baby blankets because it will help to create a softer blanket with less holes and gaps than a plain, bulky blanket. This stitch can be used in a variety of colors and patterns to create a beautiful blanket that will be treasured by the recipient.

Crochet Mitten Pattern For Beginners

A cozy and stylish pair of mittens for winter. The top is removable so that you can wear the mittens without the button closure, which can be handy when you need to answer a call on your phone or have a quick cup of coffee in the winter time.

The body of the mitten is worked in simple stitches like single crochet, but it also features a special stitch to reduce cold air entering from the bottom. It is called a foundation double crochet (fdc) and is made by ch 3 and yo, inserting the hook in the 3rd ch from your hook, yo and pull up a loop (3 loops on your hook), then yo, draw through 1 loop (1 ch made).

Crochet Mitten Pattern

To start these mittens, you will need a 3.5mm crochet hook, a 6.5mm crochet hook for the thumb and a yarn needle. You will also need a large piece of leather strip (about 7" long), either one that has been cut from an old jacket or a small strip of leather that you can purchase at your local craft store.

1. Make a cuff for the mittens with the ribbed cuff method.

With smaller hook, ch 13, leave a 6 inch tail for sewing up the seam at the end of row 2. Change to larger hook and work rows 3-4 to the short side of the cuff. Repeat these rows until the piece measures approximately 7" from the beginning and then continue on a WS row.

2. Work the thumb and wrist band as shown in this crochet mitten pattern, but attach a leather strip around the wrist using either a 1/8" hole punch or a leather punch and a nail and hammer. You can use embroidery thread to fasten the leather strip to the mitten cuffs, or you can use an adhesive adhesive.

3. Complete the mitten in these patterns as written, but use a larger needle for the cuff and a smaller needle for the thumb and wrist band.

4. Adjust the length of the body and/or thumb as needed by adding or subtracting HDC rounds between Rounds 6 - 22 of each mitten.

5. Finish off the mittens and weave in the ends.

7. When working in the round, join each new round with a slip stitch to the first stitch.

8. Work in the same manner as described for Rounds 3-6, but at the beginning of each row, sc in the same space as you joined, and work 11 sc evenly around.

With right-handed crocheters, attach the yarn to the corner of the thumb hole where Rounds 4 and 5 meet; work clockwise around the hand, sc in the same space as the join and esc in each st, including the sc at the corners, until the mitten measures approximately 4" wide by 7.5" long from the thumb opening.

Crochet Pattern For Autumn Sweater

Fall is the time of year when we start to wear our cozy sweaters and jackets. There are many patterns to choose from when it comes to crocheting an autumn sweater. You can crochet a granny square sweater, a top down raglan sweater or even a cabled sweater. All are great options for making a cozy sweater that you can wear throughout the fall season.

One of the best things about crochet is that you can easily customize the look of your sweater by choosing the right color and yarn. A lot of people will go for lighter shades like tan or yellow, but you can also choose a richer hue to make the sweater more interesting and unique.

Another way to customize the look of your crochet sweater is by using colorwork. It's a bit more challenging than a plain sweater, but if you know how to do it, you can add a whole new dimension to your crochet garment. You can even mix different colors if you want to create an even more unique crochet sweater.

You can even do a lace pattern for your crochet sweater. It's really fun to make and a great way to try out a more advanced skill level.

There are so many different ways to make a sweater, but one of the most popular ways is to use a simple raglan stitch. This type of sweater will work up quickly and is easy to customize depending on your personal style.

If you're looking for a crochet sweater pattern that's simple but stylish, then you should try this one from Carroway Crochet. It has minimal shaping and seaming and it's a great place to start if you're just getting started with your crochet journey!

This sweater is made from a fine-weight yarn, so it works up quickly and is very lightweight. It also has a very soft and comfortable feel to it. This makes it the perfect choice for a lightweight sweater that will be comfortable to wear all day long! A good tip for beginner sweater makers is to make a gauge swatch. This will help you determine how much yarn to use and what size your sweater should be in terms of length.

Once you have a gauge swatch, you can then begin to work on your sweater. It can be a little intimidating when you're first starting to work on your crochet project, but it will be worth it in the end!

It's important to follow the directions closely and measure carefully for the correct size. Taking the time to do this will ensure your sweater fits properly and will help you avoid frustration later on.

You should also be sure to read the instructions for your crochet pattern thoroughly and carefully. You may need to refer back to the instructions several times during the pattern's construction.

Once you've finished your sweater, it's time to add it to your wardrobe! You can wear it with a pair of leggings or a pair of jeans for a comfy and fashionable look. You can even dress it up a little by adding a nice belt and some cute shoes!

Chapter 5: What Every Beginner Crocheter Should Know?

If you're a beginner crocheter, then there are many things you should know before getting started. Some of these are more obvious than others, but knowing the basics will make your crochet experience much more enjoyable and help you to avoid some common pitfalls.

1. What Is Crochet?

Crochet is a great way to create items that are both functional and decorative. It's also a calming and relaxing craft that can help with mental health and mindfulness.

2. Yarns for Beginners: What You Need to Know

Not all yarns are created equal! They can vary greatly in texture, color, and fiber content. Choosing the right yarn for your project can make all the difference in how your finished product looks and feels!

3. What Are the Basic Stitches in Crochet?

If you're a new crocheter, the first pattern you should try is a simple one that uses stitches such as single crochet, half double crochet, and double crochet. These basic stitches are the foundation of most crochet patterns and will enable you to move onto more advanced patterns.

4. Crochet Stitches in Rows & Rounds: What Every Beginner Should Know

Crochet stitches are typically worked in rows, where you work your stitches across the row and then work them back over to the top of the row you just made. This can be a great way to work up your skills and increase your speed at the same time!

5. Crochet Stitches in Rounds: What Every Beginner Should Know

Another very important part of any crochet pattern is the notes section. This will tell you all of the important details about the pattern and how it's put together. It will often contain charts or stitch diagrams, and may also give you specific instructions for different sizes and materials.

6. Crochet in the Round: What Every Beginner Should Know

When learning to crochet, it can be really frustrating if you have a hard time working in the round. This is because you can easily end up with a lot of tangles and knots in your work. This is especially true if you aren't used to working in the round and don't have any previous experience with it!

7. Crochet Gauges: What Every Beginner Should Know

Crocheting gauges can be a bit confusing for beginners, as they can be very different from knitting gauges. The main thing to remember is that crochet gauges are just a guideline and not the final size of your finished project.

8. Frogging Your Project: What Every Beginner Should Know

Despite what some people might think, frogging isn't always a bad thing. If you're not too keen on a certain pattern or don't like the look of your finished piece, frogging it can be a good way to work out what went wrong and improve your skills.

9. Buying Yarn: What Every Beginner Should Know

Purchasing yarn can be very tricky for newbies to understand. You might need to ask a lot of questions in order to find the perfect yarn for your project. You'll want to make sure that you get the right weight of yarn for your project and that it comes in the correct dye lot, so that you're not getting a skein that has been dyed twice!

How to Create Impactful Designs With A Pattern Repetition

With A Pattern Repetition

A pattern is an arrangement of repeating shapes or objects that creates a visual effect. This can be a rigid, symmetrical sequence of shapes or it can be an organic and flexible form that changes with each repeated element.

There are many different ways to use patterns in your designs, and it's important to know how to use them effectively so you can create impactful designs. These techniques can be used in both print and digital art.

1. Repetition and Rhythm

When you use repetition and rhythm in your design, it will help you create a visually striking image that will catch the eye of your audience. This technique can be used to draw attention to specific elements in your design, or it can be used to help highlight key words or themes within your design.

2. Natural Repetition

One of the most common forms of repetition in nature is found in animals, birds, trees and flowers. It's often accompanied by variations, such as color or shape. You can also find repetitive patterns in art and design, such as Escher's tessellations or Ben Parker's paper sculptures.

3. Using Repetition in Photography

In photography, it's common to capture photos with repetitive objects next to each other or similar architecture that align to make an attractive composition. It's also a good idea to use a wide angle lens in order to capture more repetitions in your images, which will help you create stunning imagery.

4. Creating Repeating Lines

Another popular way to incorporate repetition into your design is by using a line. This is an easy way to add a touch of elegance to your design without adding too much text or content. This technique works best when you have a lot of empty space to work with, and it can be useful for both portrait and landscape style designs.

5. Creating Patterns Through Text

When you want to create a more dramatic effect in your design, it's sometimes necessary to use text as a background. This is an effective way to do this by creating a pattern that mimics the texture of the surrounding elements. You can use a variety of fonts to create this effect, or you can even just use your own handwriting to create the pattern.

6. Repetition In Design

The concept of repetition can be found throughout the world in art and design. You can see it in Escher's tessellations, Ben Parker's paper sculptures, and Andy Goldsworthy's radial sculptures.

7. Using Repetition in Art

Repetition is a great way to add interest and strength to your design. It's a technique that has been around since the beginning of time and is still a very popular tool in today's art scene.

8. Using Repetition in Design with a Child

When you're working with young children, it's important to use repetition to get their attention. This is a great way to engage your students and teach them how to look for patterns in the world around them.

Which Chain Should You Start With?

Whether you are new to crochet or you are an experienced crafter, you may have a project in mind that has a stitch pattern you'd like to use. The first thing you need to do is figure out how many chains you'll need to work with for your desired width of the project.

Chains are made by wrapping the yarn around your hook and then over it, with the end of the yarn that is closest to your ball resting on top. The long end of the yarn is then pulled tighter to close the loop on your hook.

If you're new to crochet, it's a good idea to start with a small project that will teach you the basics of crochet. These projects can be anything from a scarf to a blanket.

You can make a chain by working with any kind of yarn, from acrylic to wool. But it's helpful to have a hook that matches the weight of the yarn you're using, because this will improve your experience and help you get a feel for how tight or loose to make the chain.

A crochet chain looks like a series of sideways V shapes and has a small bump on the back. This is what makes it easy to count.

There are 3 ways to work into a beginning chain, and experienced crocheters often have one they prefer or will select the right method for their project. The best way to begin a project is to follow the directions in the pattern, which will tell you how many chains to skip before working into the next one.

Then, follow the instructions for your pattern to work into the second, third, etc. chain until you reach the number of stitches stated in your pattern.

It's very important to follow the pattern and not stray off the numbers in your pattern, because the stitches you're making won't match up when you get to the end of the project. It's also a good idea to check your progress against the instructions in your pattern and if you've gone off-track, just re-crochet that entire first row.

Ultimately, the correct answer to which chain you should start with will depend on what you're going to make and what kind of look you want it to have. For example, if you're making a necklace, you'll want a thicker rope chain than if you're creating a tiny cross.

The Question Of How Much Yarn To Purchase?

When you're knitting or crocheting a project, one of the most important questions is how much yarn you need. There's nothing worse than running out of yarn and having to start over or have a project that isn't finished. There are several different factors that you need to consider when deciding how much yarn you need, including the type of pattern you're working on and the thickness of the yarn.

The Weight of Yarn

When buying yarn at your local craft store, you should be able to see the weight of the yarn by looking at its label. Often, the label will show a number and the category name. These two things will tell you what weight of yarn it is and help you to know if it will be the right size for your project.

If you're not sure what the right weight of yarn is, it's best to consult a pattern before purchasing your yarn. Most patterns will have an estimate of how much yardage is needed to produce the project as written.

There are also some other useful tips to keep in mind when determining how much yarn you need for a project, including swatching and adjusting the needle size. This helps to ensure that the amount of yarn you buy will be enough for your project, even if you make changes later on.

The Thickness of the Yarn

There is a huge range of different thicknesses of yarn available for knitters to choose from. Some of these thicker yarns are perfect for shawls, while others are more appropriate for sweaters or hats.

The thickness of the yarn can change the overall look and feel of a knitted item. It can also change the amount of yarn you need to purchase, depending on whether you're making a fine garment or a coarser item.

If you want to make a lace scarf or other item that requires a lot of yarn, then it's important to use a fine or medium-weight yarn. These yarns will give you a more textured look and feel to your project, and they'll be more likely to hold up to wear over time.

Another thing to keep in mind when calculating how much yarn you need is the gauge of the fabric you're making. This can affect the amount of yarn you need to purchase, as some stitch patterns require more yarn than other types.

A skein of yarn can weigh anywhere from 1 ounce to a few pounds, so it's important to understand what the different weights of yarn are. This will allow you to determine the amount of yardage that you need for your project, so that you can get the best results possible from your knitting.

This is especially important when you're making a hat, a scarf or a blanket. These projects are typically larger than other knitted items, and they can take up a lot of yardage.

This can make it difficult to find the correct amount of yarn for a project. Thankfully, there are some handy charts that can be helpful when figuring out how much yarn you need for a particular project.

How to Secure the Ends and Weave Them in

Weaving in the ends of a project can be a tricky thing to master. Whether you're knitting, crocheting, or sewing, it's important to secure the ends so that they don't unravel with wear and washing. Weaving in the end of a piece also ensures that it looks professional and neat.

There are lots of ways to secure the ends, but there are some basic principles to follow to ensure that you have a smooth and secure finish. In addition, there are some techniques that you can use to hide the ends more discreetly.

How to Secure The Ends - Knitting

Weave in the ends of a knitting project using a tapestry needle, which will make it look professional and neat. Thread the yarn tail through the eye of the tapestry needle, and then weave it in horizontally and vertically a few times before trimming off the excess. Leave at least a 4" length on the end to weave in securely.

How to Secure The Ends -- Crochet

Weaving in the ends of a crocheted project is essential for keeping it secure and looking neat. It prevents the loose ends of yarn from coming out with wear and washing, and it also ensures that your finished item will last for years to come.

How to Weave in the Ends - Crocheting

There are some common things that you can do to keep your woven in ends secure, and they're all pretty easy to do. For starters, you need to plan where the ends will go – this is particularly important when you're working with slippery yarns or other types of fabric.

You'll want to start a new ball of yarn at the edge of your work whenever possible (this is especially useful for pieces like hats and scarves), or in a place where it will be easier to weave them in. If you have a project that involves stitching in large amounts of ends, you may want to split the yarn into several strands and weave them in separately.

Then, you need to weave in the ends of each strand in different directions so that they are less visible. The best way to do this is to weave in the ends of each strand individually before you begin blocking your finished project.

This is a very simple method, but it does require you to plan where your yarn ends will go in the final garment, as well as using a tapestry needle. This also makes it much easier to weave in the ends.

Ultimately, weaving in the ends of a crocheted piece is just one of many finishing techniques, but it's something that every knitter and crocheter should know how to do. The key is to find a technique that works for you. This will help you feel more confident in the finished piece, and it will be safer for the wearer.

What Is the Best Way to Block a Blanket?

Blocking is the process of pinning a fabric piece to shape it, usually by adding moisture and then leaving it to dry. This process can be a great way to even out tension in your work, flatten areas of curl and highlight stitch definition.

The Best Way to Block a Blanket

There are several different methods of blocking crochet pieces. The first is the method commonly known as soak blocking, which involves completely submerging the yarn in water. This method works best with natural fibres such as wool, but it can also be used with acrylic yarns.

This method requires soaking the project in water and then laying it flat on a towel to dry. It can take a few days for the wet block to fully dry.

Another option is to use spray blocking, which uses a spray bottle filled with water. This method can be done anywhere in the house, and doesn't require electricity. It does take longer to dry than steam blocking, but it's easy to use and doesn't have the risk of melting or flattening the yarn if you're not careful.

The second method of blocking is steam blocking, which involves pinning the project to a blocking board or mat and then using a garment steamer or iron to release steam onto the project. This method can be especially effective with acrylic yarns, but is a little more delicate than the other two options and needs to be done carefully.

When blocking a project, it's important to follow the care instructions for your yarn and not overly manipulate it. If you don't, it can lead to distorted stitches or a twisted project. This is especially true if you're working with acrylic or other heat-sensitive yarns, so be sure to test your method on a small swatch first.

You can also blot the block with a towel or other cloth to remove any excess moisture before pinning it in place. This is the most effective method of blocking, but it can also be tricky if you're not very experienced with it.

Whether you're blocking a large blanket or a small swatch, it's always a good idea to have a set of blocking boards and mats ready to go. These are handy because they can be shaped to the size of your project and allow you to pin it in place.

Once your blanket is pinned to the correct measurements, it's time to decide on which blocking method you'll use. There are three main options: 1.

A lot of people like to use a combination of both methods. This is a great option because it doesn't take up as much room as blocking with just one technique and can be done in any room of the house. It also allows you to use a variety of materials, including foam, to cover your boards and mats. This is a great way to save money on mats and also reduce the number of boards you need!

Chapter 6: Common Mistakes and How to Prevent Them?

Crochet is a wonderful hobby that can lead to the creation of beautiful and functional items, but even experienced crocheters can make mistakes. Here are some common mistakes and tips on how to prevent them:

1. **Tension**: Maintaining an even tension is essential for a neat and uniform stitch. Practice regularly to develop a consistent tension and use a tension gauge to help you.

With any project, it's important to have a system in place that helps you manage all of the tasks involved in delivering the product to the customer. That means assigning people to the task, making sure they have the tools and equipment to get the job done, and ensuring that all work orders make it to the right person at the right time.

The best way to do that is with a unified platform for all your work order and incident tracking needs. Having a single system that allows your team to view, track and share all of your work orders in a consolidated place will help you get more done for less time, and ultimately make the best use of everyone's efforts.

What are you waiting for? Get started today with our streamlined software solution. You'll be on your way to a more organized and efficient work order tracking program in no time!

By using the smartest tool for your needs, you can rest assured that all of the work will be completed on time and to a quality standard.

2. **Counting Stitches:** It's easy to lose track of your stitch count, especially when working on a long piece. Write down the number of stitches you make in each row, or use stitch markers to help you keep track.

3. **Missed Stitches:** This can happen when a stitch is not completed properly or when you accidentally skip a stitch. Always double-check your work and make sure each stitch is complete before moving on to the next.

4. **Incorrectly Formed Stitches:** This can happen when you insert your hook into the wrong loop or when you twist the stitch. Pay close attention to the pattern and the stitch instructions, and take your time to ensure that each stitch is formed correctly.

5. **Yarn Choice:** Choosing the right yarn for your project is important, as different yarns have different textures, thicknesses, and stretch. Always check the recommended yarn for the pattern and make sure you have enough to complete the project.

6. **Improper Finishing:** Taking the time to properly finish your work can make a big difference in the overall look of your finished item. Weave in all loose ends, and use a strong, seamless knot to secure the last stitch.

7. **Misreading the Pattern:** Crochet patterns can be confusing, especially for those who are just starting out. Always read the pattern thoroughly before starting your project and make sure you understand each stitch and symbol. Don't hesitate to ask for help or clarification if needed.

8. **Not Checking Gauge:** Checking gauge, or the number of stitches and rows per inch, is crucial for ensuring that your finished project is the correct size. Make a gauge swatch before starting your project and adjust your hook size accordingly.

Gauge (pronounced 'gage') is the word that most people use when describing a measurement tool or a unit of measure. It's a simple word that has been in use for centuries and is very familiar to most people.

Not Understanding Gauge

The first thing that you need to understand about gauge is that it's a standard. This means that it's a defined amount of weight or size that can be used to compare two items.

This is a great way to help you make sure that you're using the correct yardage for your project, and it's also an important factor in helping you get the best results from a knitting pattern. If you don't follow the recommended gauge, you can end up with a sweater that is either too big or too small.

Once you've understood the importance of a good gauge, it's time to take action and start learning more about it. You may be a knitter or you might be a business owner who uses gauge charts as part of your data storytelling process, but either way, understanding gauges is crucial to success.

There are many benefits to using gauge graphs in your business and here are some of the main reasons why:

A Gauge Chart Template is a great way to show how customers feel about their experience with your business over a period of time, including how they're resolving issues or dealing with their concerns. This type of dashboard is a great way to collect feedback on your service level and to make strategic decisions based on it.

Getting Gauge Swatches Right

When you're making a sweater, for example, the most important thing is to make sure that your gauge matches the designer's. You can't always be sure that you're following the same stitch pattern as the designer, but if your gauge is correct, it's unlikely that you will run out of yarn before you're finished the whole project.

Having gauge is also important when choosing the right kind of yarn for a project. There are many different types of fibers and it's not uncommon for some fibers to be thicker than others, so you'll want to be sure that you're using the appropriate type.

Gauge swatches are the best place to start when it comes to deciding on yarn because you'll be able to see exactly how much yarn you're going to need. Then, you can decide whether or not you'd like to stick with that particular type of yarn or if you should move onto something else.

Another great advantage of having gauge swatches is that you can easily swap out the yarn for a different one when it's time to make your sweater. This gives you the freedom to choose a yarn that's a better fit for your needs and your budget.

This is an easy and fun activity that helps you understand the difference between a gauge and a gage. You can even have a competition to see which one you can remember most of the time!

9. **Not Keeping Track of the Right Side:** Some patterns require that you work on a specific side, either the right or the wrong side. Make sure to keep track of which side you are working on and mark it if necessary.

10. **Not Blocking Your Work:** Blocking is a process of wetting, shaping and drying your finished crochet item to give it a polished and finished look. Always check the pattern instructions to see if blocking is required, and follow proper blocking techniques to ensure that your project turns out perfectly.

By being mindful of these common mistakes and taking the necessary steps to prevent them, you can improve your crochet skills and enjoy the process of creating beautiful and functional pieces.

Conclusion

Crochet is a wonderful hobby that can be both relaxing and productive. It's a great way to create beautiful and unique items using just a few basic stitches. Whether you're making a scarf, a blanket, or a hat, crochet is an easy and satisfying way to get started with a new crafting project.

For beginners, it's important to start with simple projects and basic stitches. This will help you get the hang of the basic movements and give you the confidence to try more complex patterns. Once you've mastered the basics, you can move on to more intricate patterns and designs.

Crochet is also a great hobby for those who are looking for a way to be creative, express their artistic side, and make something that is truly unique. Whether you're making items for yourself, friends, or family, crochet is a great way to bring joy and beauty into your life and the lives of others.

Overall, crochet is a wonderful hobby that can be both fun and rewarding. Whether you're a beginner or an experienced crocheter, there is always something new to learn and create with this versatile craft.

Printed in Great Britain
by Amazon

18956802R00068